William Bodine

Judges and *Kings:* *God's Chosen Leaders*

WILLIAM N. McELRATH • ILLUSTRATED BY CLIFF JOHNSTON

BROADMAN PRESS
Nashville, Tennessee

4242-49
ISBN: 0-8054-4249-9

Dewey Decimal Classification: J220.91
Subject headings: JUDGES, BIBLICAL//KINGS, BIBLICAL

Printed in the United States of America.

Contents

Gideon: Captain Who Obeyed God's Orders

Gideon was hiding. Secretly he carried wheat to the place where grapes were stored. There he beat the stalks to knock loose the golden grains.

In other years Gideon had hauled his wheat to an open hilltop. There he had driven oxen over the stalks.

But not any more—not since the days of the desert raiders. Every year as crops were harvested, the raiders swooped in from the east. All of the cows, sheep, and donkeys were herded away. The raiders burned and slashed and looted. Again Gideon's family had nothing left to eat.

Suddenly Gideon looked up from

beating the wheat. How had a stranger found his secret place?

The stranger spoke, "God is with you, O brave and mighty man!"

Brave? When Gideon was hiding?

Mighty? When neither he nor anyone else could fight off the desert raiders?

Gideon shook his head. "If God is with us, why has all this happened?"

Then Gideon began to realize that the stranger was God's messenger. "Rescue your people from the raiders," the messenger urged. "You can do it because I will help you."

It took awhile for Gideon to believe. At last he felt sure. Lifting a twisted ram's horn, he blew a great blast.

Down from the hills, up from the valleys, even from across the river, men tramped in to join Gideon's army.

Then came strange orders from God: "Gideon, you have too many men."

Maybe Gideon wondered whether he had somehow gotten God's message backward: Not too many men, but too few!

5

The enemy had four times as many
soldiers as he.

But Gideon obeyed God's orders.
"Who's afraid?" he cried to his men. "If
you're afraid, go back home."

Twenty-two thousand men left. Only
ten thousand stayed. But God wasn't

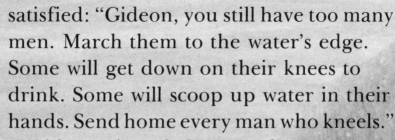

satisfied: "Gideon, you still have too many men. March them to the water's edge. Some will get down on their knees to drink. Some will scoop up water in their hands. Send home every man who kneels."

Gideon obeyed God's orders, even though only three hundred men were left.

"When you beat the desert raiders," God
explained, "everyone must know that it is
through God's strength, not your own."

Across a broad valley stretched the tents
of the desert raiders. They looked like
swarming locusts.

Gideon went scouting with another
man. Hiding outside a tent, he heard an

enemy soldier tell a strange dream: "A loaf of barley bread rolled into camp and smashed a tent."

"I know what that means," gasped another warrior. "It means Gideon and his troops will beat us."

Gideon crept away, glad to know the raiders were afraid of him.

Now Captain Gideon laid battle plans. To every soldier he handed a ram's horn

and a flaming torch in a clay jar to hide its
light. He divided his tiny army into three
combat teams and gave his orders.

Black midnight came, and the desert
raiders were changing the guard.
Suddenly their camp was ringed with fire!
And from hills all around came an

ear-splitting blast. Three hundred voices cried, "A sword for the Lord and for Gideon!"

The raiders panicked. In the dark every man fought his neighbor. They tripped over tent ropes in a mad rush to the camels. Few of them got away.

Gideon made sure they wouldn't come back. He chased them into the hills. He captured their kings.

"Be our king!" begged the people who had followed Gideon. "You have saved us from the desert raiders."

Gideon shook his head. "I will not be your king," he said. "God is your king!"

And all the years that Captain Gideon led them, his people faithfully obeyed God's orders.

Thinkback: Can you draw three things Gideon used to beat the raiders?

Why did God order Captain Gideon to send most of his men home?

Samson: Strongman Who Wasted God's Gifts

Samson grew up knowing he was special. Time and again his mother told him his favorite story: "After all my childless years, God's angel promised me a son. And when your father sacrificed a goat on the rock altar, the angel rose toward heaven in the flames."

Samson's father and mother never saw the angel again. But they remembered his orders: The boy Samson was to let his hair grow long. That was one way people in those days showed they had been promised to God.

His parents remembered with hope the

13

angel's promise: "Samson will begin the work of rescuing God's people from the Philistines."

Sorrow shadowed their hearts the day Samson blurted out, "There's a Philistine girl I like—in Timnah, down the valley. Get her for my wife!"

As he stalked through the vineyards toward Timnah, Samson heard a young lion roaring. With his bare hands he tore the life out of it.

A few days later, Samson saw that wild bees had swarmed in the lion's carcass. His hands dripped honey when he arrived for his wedding feast.

"Come, let's play riddles!" Samson cried over the wine cups. "The loser must pay thirty suits of fine clothes. 'Out of the eater came something to eat; Out of the strong came something sweet.'"

None of the Philistines could guess Samson's riddle about the honey from the lion. So they threatened his bride with death unless she learned the secret.

After three days of nagging, Samson

gave in. So at the end of the week-long
wedding feast, the Philistine guests won
their wager.

Samson was angry. Off he raged to
another Philistine town eight leagues
away. There he killed thirty men and
looted their wardrobes to pay off his bet.

The fears of Samson's parents proved

true: Trying to marry a heathen Philistine brought nothing but trouble. The girl and her father died by fire before all was done. But Samson brought both fire and sword on the Philistines in revenge.

Samson made camp at a cave in the hills of Dan. For twenty years his name grew to be a legend, as he led God's people to victory over their enemies.

Once he slaughtered a thousand men with no weapon but the jawbone of a donkey. Once he yanked up the gates of Gaza, a Philistine stronghold, and carried them thirteen leagues across the hills to Hebron.

But too often Samson swaggered out looking for women to win, not for foes to fight. And it was a woman, Delilah, who finally did him in.

"Tell me what makes you so strong!" Delilah teased him. At first he teased her in turn with false answers.

She tried tying him up with seven new bowstrings. Next it was new ropes, never used before. Both times he snapped the

16

knots like thread. Then he made her believe he would weaken if she wove his long hair into her loom. But he broke free.

Finally Samson admitted that he had been promised to God from birth. "Cut my hair," said he, "and I'll be as weak as anybody else."

Delilah had Samson's hair cut while he slept. Then the Philistines pounced on him, gouged out his eyes, and set him to grinding grain in Gaza like a donkey.

Too late he realized how he had wasted God's gifts. "Lord, let me have revenge just this once!" he pleaded. In prison his hair grew and his strength returned.

One day the five Philistine kings

18

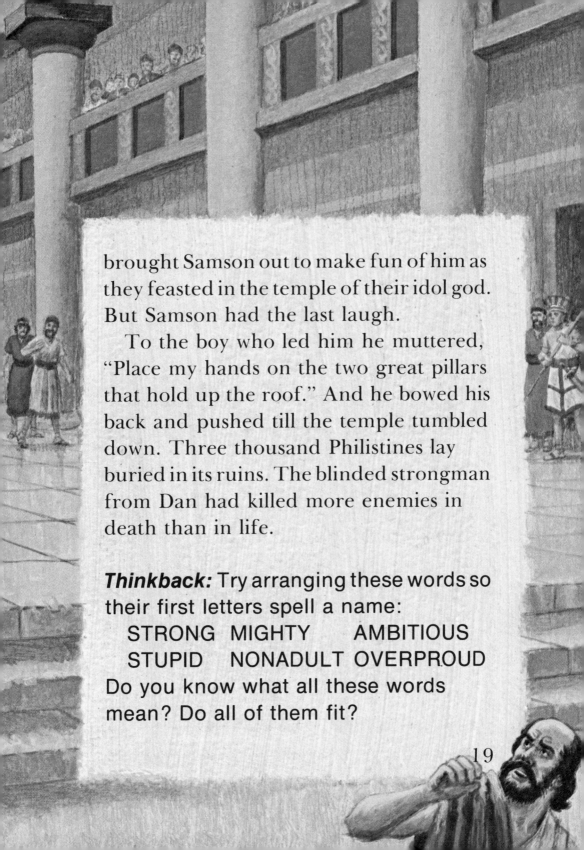

brought Samson out to make fun of him as they feasted in the temple of their idol god. But Samson had the last laugh.

To the boy who led him he muttered, "Place my hands on the two great pillars that hold up the roof." And he bowed his back and pushed till the temple tumbled down. Three thousand Philistines lay buried in its ruins. The blinded strongman from Dan had killed more enemies in death than in life.

Thinkback: Try arranging these words so their first letters spell a name:

STRONG MIGHTY AMBITIOUS
STUPID NONADULT OVERPROUD

Do you know what all these words mean? Do all of them fit?

19

Solomon: Wise King in Wealthy Times

Solomon, son of King David, nearly missed being king at all. An older brother claimed the throne when King David was very old. But David commanded that young Solomon be made king.

So Solomon rode the royal mule with the royal bodyguard beside him. Trumpets and pipes shrilled. And all the people shouted: "Long live King Solomon!"

After David's death, the new king left
Jerusalem to worship at a nearby hilltop
shrine. There God spoke to him in a
dream: "What will you have as my gift?"

Solomon well knew how young and
inexperienced he was. "Give me wisdom,
O Lord," he begged. "How can I ever rule
your people without your wisdom?"

This answer pleased God. Not only did
he give what Solomon had asked for but he
also gave him wealth and honor. "And if
you obey me as your father David did," he
added, "I will give you long life."

Wisdom and wealth! Who can say which
King Solomon had more of?

There was no doubt about his wisdom.
People never stopped talking about hard

21

cases he had settled.

Solomon composed songs and proverbs by the thousands. He studied herbs and trees, birds and beasts. Foreign kings told of his wisdom. The queen of Sheba came from the south and confessed, "They didn't tell me half the truth."

As to wealth, whether you measured it in gold or grain, cattle or chariots, Solomon was rich beyond all counting. He stabled

his horses in cities throughout the land. His ships brought treasure from distant ports. And tribute poured in from the river Euphrates to the Great Sea, from Syria to the borders of Egypt.

Certainly Solomon needed all his wealth for what he set out to do. He built the Lord's Temple, fulfilling David's fondest dream. He also built the most magnificent palaces Jerusalem had ever seen. Gold and ivory adorned his throne. Twelve

sculptured lions guarded its steps.

Solomon built one special palace for an Egyptian princess who became his wife. But he didn't stop there—either in marrying or in building. He took hundreds of wives. Many came from foreign countries his father had conquered. And for them Solomon also built shrines, so they could worship their foreign gods.

Both wealth and wisdom began to fail the king in his later years. To pay for cedar logs rafted down the coast from Lebanon, Solomon had to give up twenty towns in Galilee. To finish his building projects, he drafted his own people into forced labor.

Cracks widened in the greatness of Solomon's kingdom. Raiders attacked, from Edom to the south and from Damascus to the north. One of Solomon's own officials rebelled against him and ran away to go on plotting in Egypt.

Yet no other king could match the wealth and wisdom of Solomon. Even Jesus spoke many centuries later of "Solomon in all his glory"!

Thinkback: Do you remember *what* Jesus said when he talked about "Solomon in all his glory"? Read Matthew 6:29.

What do you think was the greatest thing Solomon did during his reign? Which of his many building projects was most famous and most important?

Joash: True King in Troubled Times

Joash never knew what it was like to play as other boys did. He was the true king of Judah, and he was in hiding.

Joash couldn't remember the terrible day when news came that his father was dead. That day two kings, one queen, and many princes died. Joash escaped because his aunt had picked him up and had run to a secret room in the Temple.

There young Joash had lived ever since. No one knew he was there except his nursemaid, his aunt, and her husband, the high priest.

Joash never played outdoors. The high priest feared that the cruel queen would murder Joash too.

All of that changed one sabbath day when Joash was seven years old. The high priest laid careful plans. Temple watchmen who usually went home stayed on duty that day. When the new sentries marched in, a royal bodyguard of double strength was formed.

From a hidden place the priest brought spears and shields. Joash knew those arms had once belonged to his six-greats grandfather, mighty King David.

"Here is the true king!" the high priest proclaimed. Trumpets blared.

"Long live King Joash!" shouted the guards. Joash felt the weight of the crown of Judah as the high priest gently placed it on his head.

Queen Athaliah stalked in. "Treason! Treason!" she screamed. But soon swords had put an end forever to Joash's wicked grandmother.

And so the true king came to his throne. He listened to the wise old high priest and tried his best to be as good a king as David.

29

Many tasks called for King Joash's attention. One job was repairing the Temple. Athaliah had used it as a place to worship heathen gods.

So King Joash called the priests. "Use gifts of gold and silver that worshipers bring to make God's house beautiful once again," he said.

But times were still troubled. The king found that even some of God's priests were cheaters. He and the old high priest had to have a special box made. Offerings

brought to the Temple were dropped through a hole in the top.

Now no greedy priest could sneak out any money. Soon carpenters, masons, and stonecutters swarmed over the Temple.

The most troubled times of all came after the old high priest died. King Joash had grown up by now. He listened to new counselors. Some gave him bad advice. When the high priest's son tried to warn the king, Joash even ordered him killed.

The end came much like the beginning. The king of Syria attacked Jerusalem. In the battle King Joash was badly wounded. As he lay helpless on his bed, two palace officials murdered him.

He was buried in the royal tombs of the City of David. Nearby lay the old high priest who had crowned Joash as true king so many years before.

Thinkback: Can you list two things that helped Joash be a good king?

Can you list many *more* things that made it hard for him to be a good king?

Hezekiah: Ruler Who Trusted God

King Hezekiah was a good son of a bad father. King Ahaz had sacrificed to idols. He even closed the Lord's Temple. But Hezekiah opened the Temple again. He

had it cleaned and repaired. He invited people from all over his kingdom and from other tribes to join in worship there.

Hezekiah discovered the bronze snake made by Moses in the desert hundreds of years before. It had been kept all this time. How sad Moses would have been to see God's people burning incense to it! King Hezekiah ordered it broken to bits.

None of his good deeds seemed to help, though, when Hezekiah got sick. The prophet Isaiah warned him: "God says, 'Get ready to die.' "

Hezekiah was far from old. He was far from finished with what he had hoped to do as king. No wonder he wept as he turned his face to the wall and prayed!

The Lord heard Hezekiah's cry for help. Before Isaiah had left the palace grounds, he got new orders. Walking back to the royal bedroom, he prophesied: "O king, God has given you fifteen more years to live. In three days you will be well enough to worship in the Temple."

Hezekiah was glad, but he found it hard

33

to believe. "What sign from God will prove your words?" he asked.

"You may choose," said Isaiah. "Your father Ahaz built a stairway to measure the shadow cast by the sun. Shall the shadow go ten steps forward or ten steps back?"

Hezekiah chose ten steps back because he knew it was harder. The miracle

35

happened. And so did quick healing.

Such experiences with God helped Hezekiah when his kingdom was attacked by the emperor of Assyria. He built stronger walls with towers around Jerusalem. He stopped up springs outside the city and brought water into it through a tunnel in solid rock. He ordered spears and shields made. He gathered all his men at the city gate. But still he told them: "Our best defense is our trust in God."

Three Assyrian army commanders
strutted up to Jerusalem. "Where's
Hezekiah?" they demanded.

The king stayed home. He sent instead
three of his own officers.

"What makes Hezekiah think he can
hold out?" demanded the Assyrians.
"What makes him think his God is any
stronger than the gods of all the other
nations we've conquered?"

"Ssh! Not so loud," begged King Hezekiah's officials. "People sitting on the city walls can hear you."

The proud Assyrians shouted even louder: "Our message is for all of you! You

will all starve to death if you don't surrender. Don't let Hezekiah or his God try to fool you!"

No one answered a word. Hezekiah had wisely ordered silence. When he heard what had happened, the king tore his clothes in grief and hurried to the Temple.

A change in the fortunes of war caused the Assyrians to move farther away from Jerusalem. But the emperor didn't want anybody to think he was through. He sent a letter to Hezekiah. In it he insulted Hezekiah and Hezekiah's God.

Once more Hezekiah turned toward the Temple. There he spread out the letter. "O Lord," he prayed, "you know what it says. Rescue us, for we trust in you!"

Isaiah sent the king a comforting message: "The Assyrian emperor will never enter this city. He will not even shoot an arrow into it."

That very night, death struck down tens of thousands in the Assyrian army. The emperor hurried back home without most of his army.

Is it any wonder that good King Hezekiah trusted God all his days?

Thinkback: Hezekiah built a _ _ _ _ _ tunnel in Jerusalem which is still there today. But something else about Hezekiah proved even more permanent: His _ _ _ _ _ in God.

Josiah: Ruler Who Returned to God

The rulers of God's people had gone from bad to worse. After two wicked kings, father and son, an eight-year-old grandson came to the throne.

Yet that little boy, Josiah, grew up to become one of the greatest and best rulers of God's people. When he was sixteen, he began to worship the Lord. When he was twenty, he began to clear away signs of idol worship left by his father and grandfather.

By the time King Josiah was twenty-six, the Temple was cleansed of idols. But the ancient house of worship sagged with the weight of years.

Josiah ordered the royal secretary, "Go to the Temple. Count the money there. Use it to buy timber and stone. Hire masons and carpenters to repair the house of God."

The secretary obeyed. Returning to the palace, he reported all he had done. Then he added surprising news: "The high

priest gave me this book of the Law which
he found in the Temple."

Josiah pointed toward the scroll in the
secretary's hand. "Read it."

Not long after the reading began, the
young king tore his robes as a sign of grief.
"Go to the prophetess Huldah," he
commanded. "Ask her what God will do to
us because we have not obeyed his Law."

Huldah prophesied that God would
indeed punish his people. But she added

42

one note of comfort: "Tell the man who
sent you that he himself has listened to me
and obeyed me. Punishment will not come
as long as he is still your king."

Josiah called all his people to a special
meeting in the Temple. There the king
himself read from the book of the Law.

Then priest and Levite, rich and poor
joined Josiah in pledging to return to God.
   In the book Josiah read how the
Passover should be observed. He ordered
the biggest celebration of that annual holy
day ever held since the days of Samuel.
From all over his realm people came to

Jerusalem for a week of worship.

For many years Josiah ruled in peace. Then came a time when the Pharaoh of Egypt hurried to join Josiah's enemies. Josiah led his army. But Egyptian arrows found their mark in his body.

"Take me away; I'm badly hurt!" he

groaned. The royal chariot rumbled back toward Jerusalem. Soon after it arrived, the king lay dead.

Great was the mourning for Josiah. For Huldah's prophecy proved true: In twenty-three years three of Josiah's sons and one of his grandsons briefly wore the crown in Jerusalem. They were the last kings to rule God's people there for centuries to come.

Thinkback: Would you like to read the book of God's Law which was found in the Temple? Probably it was part of the book of _ E _ _ E _ O _ O _ _.

What bad news and what good news did King Josiah hear from the prophetess?

46

Reflections

Use numbers to show which of God's chosen leaders fits each description:

1) Gideon   3) Solomon 5) Hezekiah
2) Samson 4) Joash   6) Josiah

Two who had bad parents: __, __
Two who had bad grandparents: __, __
Two who became rulers as boys: __, __
Three whom some people might call
   failures: They died by violence, their
   tasks unfinished: __, __, __

If these six chosen leaders of God's people could give you good advice today, which one do you think would say each of the following sentences?

__ "Obey God, no matter what."
__ "Trust God, no matter what."
__ "Ask God for wisdom."
__ "Let God's spokesman guide you."
__ "Keep God's Law always."
__ "Use God's gifts wisely."

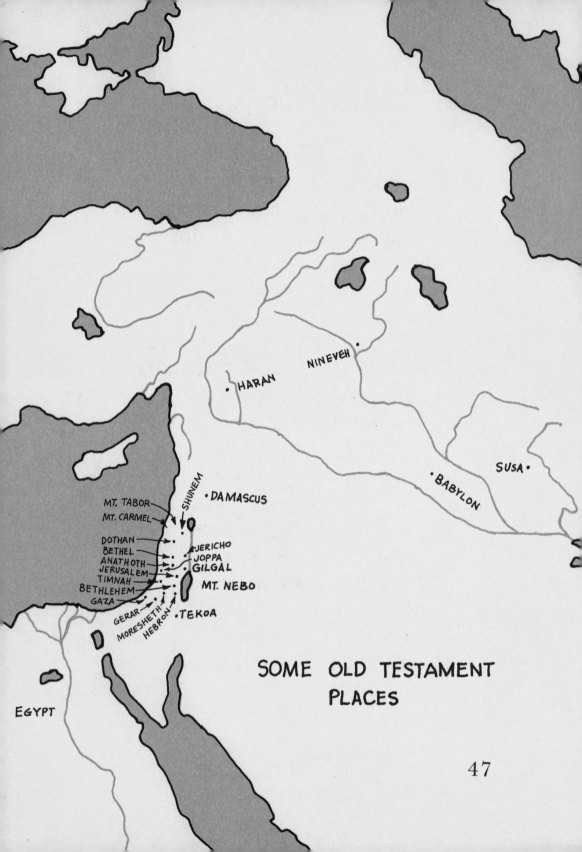

HARAN

NINEVEH

SUSA •

• BABYLON

SHUNEM

MT. TABOR
MT. CARMEL

• DAMASCUS

DOTHAN
BETHEL
ANATHOTH
JERUSALEM
TIMNAH
BETHLEHEM
GAZA

• JERICHO
JOPPA
GILGAL

MT. NEBO

GERAR
MORESHETH
HEBRON

• TEKOA

EGYPT

SOME OLD TESTAMENT
PLACES

47